THE YOUNG ENTREPRENEURS FINANCIAL LITERACY HANDBOOK

DEBORAH REYNOLDS

Author: Deborah Reynolds

Photo Images: iStockphoto.com, and Edward Reynolds

Paperback ISBN: 978-0-9903831-7-8

Email; dreynolds@futuremogulsic.com

Published in the USA.

A WORD FROM THE AUTHOR

The Young Entrepreneurs Financial Literacy Handbook Name Image Likeness (NIL) Athletes Edition is written to support young college athletes who because of hard work and dedication to their sport have been selected to benefit from the new NIL policy. They will now be compensated for their college performance instead of having to wait until they are possibly selected by a professional sports team. Considering the number of professional teams representing each sport, the number of players on each team, and the number of college athletes, the probability of reaching the professional level is quite low.

Even though the focus is on NIL athletes and policy, anyone can benefit from the information found on the pages of this book. Care was taken to make it easy to read and understand. During these times everyone can benefit from financial literacy.

In organizing this book, I concentrated on five major units: NIL policy, financial management (personal finance), banking, investing, and entrepreneurship. Under each unit are related topics.

Each topic begins with **objectives** for learning. For some topics there is an **essential question** which does not have a right or wrong answer but gives the reader something to think about as they go through the topic. The **warm-up** gets the reader to think about the new topic or review the previous topic. **Lesson highlights** provide key information on each topic along with definitions. The **activities** reinforce comprehension of the information presented. It can also be used as an assessment. Sometimes there is a **tip** the reader can use to help them move towards a successful future.

There is also a **Next Meeting** assignment to complete before moving on to the next topic.

Finally, readers are encouraged to use search engines such as Google, ChatGPT, Bing, Yahoo, DuckDuckGo, and Ecosia. They can help in research and answer mathematical problems.

TABLE OF CONTENTS

UNIT 1

TOPIC 1
NAME IMAGE LIKENESS (NIL) POLICY

OBJECTIVES

Reader will be able to:

- Describe the function of the NCAA.
- Explain the purpose of the NIL policy.
- List benefits of the policy and its impact on collegiate sports.
- Identify controversies in the policy.
- Research perspectives of policy by those impacted by the policy.
- Identify 5 collegiate athletes in different sports who have benefitted from the policy.

ESSENTIAL QUESTION

Five years from now will NIL have had a positive or negative effect on college sports, and will there ever be equality in the application of this policy?

_____

_____

_____

_____

_____

_____

_____

_____

_____

_____

WARMUP

Name four activities an athlete can engage in and receive NIL compensation.

1.
_____
_____
_____
_____
_____

2.
_____
_____
_____
_____
_____

3.
_____
_____
_____
_____
_____

4.
_____
_____
_____
_____
_____

LESSON HIGHLIGHTS

The **National Collegiate Athletic Association (NCAA)** is a nonprofit organization whose purpose is to regulate college sports and provide a successful and meaningful experience for college students. It was founded in 1906 to protect student athletes from the brutality that often occurred in some sports such as football.

As of this writing the NCAA covers 24 sports, nearly 1100 schools, and over 500,000 college athletes. There are three divisions. The largest schools belong to Division I. The three divisions are also divided into subdivisions. Its headquarters are in Indianapolis, Indiana.

The **Name Image Likeness Policy (NIL)** was adopted by the NCAA on June 30, 2021. It provides guidelines for college athletes by which they can be compensated monetarily for use of their name, image, or likeness for marketing campaigns and promoting their brand. It includes such activities as autograph signing, starting a business, giving speeches, and using their social media accounts to sell products. However, as of this writing schools are starting to pay athletes. Some payments will be in the form of trusts.

NIL has become an ever-growing monolith which is turning collegiate sports upside down. The policy is the result of a unanimous Supreme Court ruling against the NCAA in which they cannot limit the money paid to college athletes because of federal antitrust regulations. A new division of the NCAA is being proposed. This is the result of the extremely profitable tv and media income.

Opinions towards the policy are diverse with pros and cons. The most positive effect is that student collegiate athletes can now receive compensation for such activities as personal appearances, autographs, merchandise endorsements, public speaking, podcasts, blogging, music, art, camps, and NFTs (nonfungible tokens) which is a type of investment. They receive compensation sometimes from collectives which are groups of school supporters who pool their money together. With the recent changes and schools starting to compensate athletes, the influence of booster clubs and collectives may be diminished

A big negative of this policy is that it is not universally applied. Not every state has signed the policy into law. Also, even though a state has permitted the policy, the rules can vary among its colleges. An athlete must know the rules before applying for NIL.

Consequently, many legislatures are pushing Congress for a federal policy for more clarity. Congress has been reluctant to address this issue. Finally, down the road there will be many changes to this policy. In some states it can be applied to high school students.

TIP: Athletes and their parents must do their best to research schools and reach out to school officials before applying for entrance.

ACTIVITY

Explain the function of the NCAA in college sports.

_____

_____

_____

_____

_____

_____

_____

_____

_____

In what ways has NIL changed college sports?

_____

_____

_____

_____

_____

_____

_____

_____

UNIT 2

TOPIC 2

UNDERSTANDING THE PURPOSE OF MONEY AND HOW IT IS REPRESENTED

Unit 2 consists of several topics which introduce the reader to the purpose of money, different denominations and currencies, how to shop wisely, budgets, and the importance of good credit. This unit contains activities and assessments to reinforce student comprehension of these topics.

OBJECTIVES

- If you want to become rich you should be able to:
- Identify and represent different money denominations.
- Count money using as few coins and bills as possible.
- Read and write numbers using dollars and cents.
- Understand the purpose of money and how it affects the economy
- Investigate Cryptocurrency and what distinguishes it from other money denominations.
- Explain the purpose of the Federal Reserve.
- State why cryptocurrency has become widely used and valuable.

WARM-UP: WHAT IS YOUR MONEY IQ?

1. **What are the Benjamins?**

   _____

   _____

   _____

   _____

   _____

2. **What are "Dead Presidents"?**

   _____

   _____

   _____

   _____

   _____

3. Before money, what system was used to pay for goods and services

_____

_____

_____

_____

_____

LESSON HIGHLIGHTS

Before money, people bartered or traded to obtain any goods or services they needed. For example, an auto mechanic may fix an accountants car in exchange for getting his income tax return prepared. This barter system is still used today by a few people.

Today coins and bills are used because a standard unit of value is needed. They are also easier to carry. Coins are no longer made of all copper or silver metal, but rather a combination of copper and nickel. Coin denominations and values are the penny (1cent), nickel (5cents), dime (10cents), quarter (25cents), half-dollar (50cents), and dollar (100cents). The bills or paper money denominations are $1, $2, $5, $10, $20, $50, and $100.

Paper money is also called Federal Reserve notes. The Federal Reserve is a government agency which controls the supply of money and interest rates banks can charge lenders when they want to borrow money. The actions of the Federal Reserve impacts management of resources or the economy of the United States and the world.

The Federal Reserve can raise or lower prime lending rates (the lowest interest rates) to protect investors. Cryptocurrency was first introduced in 2008 with Bitcoin which is still the largest and most expensive currency. It is a digital currency in which many people have invested. Some other cryptocurrencies are Ethereum, Litecoin, Tether, USD Coin, Binance Coin, Solana, and Dogecoin. There are others. Before investing it is always important to do research.

Cryptocurrency can be purchased at online exchanges such as Coinbase and Webull. To keep track of all transactions a technology called a **blockchain** is used to keep transactions secure. The blockchain acts as a balance sheet. Because it is not controlled by the government, illegal transactions have occurred.

ACTIVITY 1

Complete the following chart using real or fake money. You may also research the answers using the internet. The first column lists the various monetary denominations. Looking at both sides identify the famous person on one side and the famous place or symbol on the other side.

Denomination	Famous Person	Famous Place/Symbol
Penny		
Nickel		
Dime		
Quarter		
Half-Dollar		
Silver Dollar		
$1		
$2		
$5		
$10		
$20		
$50		
$100		

ACTIVITY 2

Answer each question below and tell how many of each type of money denomination would represent your answer using the least number of coins and bills.

1. Write twelve hundred fifty eight dollars and sixty nine cents using the dollar sign and a decimal point.

Pennies	Nickels	Dimes	Quarters	$1	$5	$10	$20	$100

2. Kevin purchased five games for $29.99 each plus an additional tax of 7%. He gave the cashier two-hundred-dollar bills. How much change did he get back?

NEXT MEETING

Select five items to buy at the mall. Bring pictures and prices. If coupons are available bring those also.

_____

_____

_____

_____

_____

_____

_____

_____

_____

_____

TOPIC 3
SPENDING MONEY WISELY

OBJECTIVES

In order to achieve financial success in sports, an athlete must start to plan early and be able to:

- Distinguish between wants and needs.
- Distinguish income from expense items.
- Prepare a budget.
- List advantages and disadvantages of cash purchases versus credit card purchases.

ESSENTIAL QUESTION

Does having a lot of money make you more likely to be happy?

_____

_____

_____

_____

_____

_____

_____

_____

_____

_____

WARM-UP

Write below five items on your shopping list and check whether they are a want or need.

SHOPPING LIST

	ITEM	WANT	NEED
1			
2			
3			
4			
5			

LESSON HIGHLIGHTS

Money is a tool which allows us to obtain the things we need. We can buy food, clothing, cars, and homes. We can buy the latest technology in computers, phones, and games. We can take vacations and eat in restaurants. Money allows us to become independent and not depend on others to supply our needs. Money allows us to have more self-esteem.

No matter how much money we make, we should always control the amount we spend. To accumulate wealth, we must always spend less than we make and make wise purchases. We should distinguish between wants and needs, and refrain from too much impulsive spending. Impulsive spending happens often during the holiday seasons, especially Christmas. We should also look for sales and use coupons to reduce the items regular or original price. When purchasing food, it is wise to buy in bulk, or more than one of each item. Large warehouse outlets such as Costco, BJ's and Sam's Club are popular places for buying in bulk. They package items such as ketchup and toothpaste with two or three in a package. The package usually shows the unit price (price of one) and total price.

When shopping we can pay using cash, debit card, or credit card. Cash is usually best, but many times credit cards are used when you don't have cash or a debit card. Unfortunately, some businesses will no longer take cash. This has occurred in retail food businesses in airports.

A credit card is a type of bank loan. You can make a purchase today and pay later. However, if you do not pay the purchase amount within thirty days the bank will charge you an additional amount called **interest**. Thus a $300 television set bought using a credit card could end up costing you much more depending on the interest rate and the length of time you take paying off the credit card.

Interest rates have skyrocketed in recent years. Monthly interest rates are close to 35% on many store credit cards and close to 25% on bank credit cards. This can have a major impact on your ability to pay off your debt and lower your credit score, which will be discussed later.

ACTIVITIES

1. Complete the following table and calculate the unit price (price of one unit of measure).

Unit price = Price ÷ Number of Units

Item & Size	Price	Unit Price
Ketchup A -40 oz.	$4.10	Per oz.
Ketchup B – 12 0z.	$2.38	Per oz.

Which ketchup is the best deal? _____

2. Macy's is having a special sale on Wednesday and will reduce the price of ladies and men watches. An Apple watch that regularly sales for $360 will be reduced by 15%. What will be the sales price before tax is added? _____

NEXT MEETING

Write about something you dream of having or doing.

_____

_____

_____

_____

_____

_____

_____

_____

_____

_____

TOPIC 4

DREAMS VERSUS GOALS AND BUDGETS

OBJECTIVES

To have a long successful career in the sports world, an athlete must:

1. Develop short- and long-term goals.
2. Distinguish between wants and needs
3. Distinguish income from expense items
4. Prepare a budget

LESSON HIGHLIGHTS

Goals are objectives that we work towards achieving. They may be **short-term goals** which can be achieved in less than three months. Examples are exercising 20 minutes daily for a month; saving money for an upcoming concert ticket; and increasing store sales 10% over last month's sales.

Intermediate goals are those which can be achieved within 3 months to a year. Saving for a car down payment or a new computer is an intermediate goal. **Long-term goals** take longer than a year to achieve. Purchasing a home or business is a long-term goal.

No matter what type of goal you set, they should be **SMART** (specific, measurable, attainable, realistic, and timely).

To achieve a goal, it is important to create and write a personal goal statement. This statement helps you understand what the goal is about and why it is important to you.

This process helps you select a time frame and keep focused.

BUDGETS

To achieve our financial goals, it is important that we prepare a **budget** which serves as the foundation of any financial plan.

A **budget** is a financial statement written for a future period. It shows your **income/revenue** (where your money comes from) or how much you have and your **expenses** (where your money goes). A budget shows the best way to distribute these funds.

Personal budgets are very important because they help us keep personal spending under control and allow us to save and reach short-term and long-term goals. The importance of a budget should be taught at an early age when children start receiving an allowance. Managing money becomes a habit and easily translates into becoming an adult managing a business budget. The following page is an example of a personal monthly budget. It lists all the names and amounts of money coming into the home each month and the names and amounts of money or expenses that must be paid out each month. By preparing a budget one can make the necessary adjustments so that the expenses are always less than the income.

BUDGET   Month _____ Year

INCOME:

Wages/Tips	$ 5,280.00
Interest income	$ 2.00
Other Income	$ 250.00
Total Income	**$ 5,532.00**

EXPENSES:

Savings	$ 200.00
Rent/Mortgage	$ 1,670.00
Health Insurance	$ 320.00
Car Payment	$ 360.00
Car Insurance	$ 225.00
Utilities	$ 230.00
Phone	$ 146.00
Cable	$ 87.00
Credit Cards/Store Accounts	$ 180.00
School Loans	$ 260.00
Groceries	$ 400.00
Transportation/Gas	$ 230.00
Laundry/Cleaners	$ 128.00
Clothing/Hair Allowance	$ 225.00
Entertainment	$ 240.00
Gifts	$ 5.00
Other Expenses	$ 200.00
Total Expenses	**$ 5,106.00**

In the table below place the dollar amount of each item in either the income or expense column. When completed calculate the total the total for the income and total for the expenses.

	ITEM	INCOME	EXPENSE
1	Allowance $100/month		
2	Cell phone $95/month		
3	Payroll check $2600/month		
4	Rent $850/month		
5	Cable and internet $193/month		
	TOTALS		

What is the **net income** (income – expenses)? _____

Help your parents prepare a monthly budget using the following chart.

BUDGET FOR MONTH OF _____

INCOME	AMOUNT
WAGES/TIPS	
INTEREST INCOME	
OTHER INCOME	
TOTAL INCOME	
EXPENSES	
SAVINGS	
RENT/MORTGAGE	
GAS, ELECTRIC, & CABLE	
CAR PAYMENT & TRANSPORTATION	
HEALTH INSURANCE & AUTO INSURANCE	
CABLE	
CREDIT CARDS	
GROCERIES	
CLOTHING/HAIR/ENTERTAINMENT	
OTHER EXPENSES	
TOTAL EXPENSES	
NET INCOME	

TOPIC 5

THE IMPORTANCE AND WISE USE OF CREDIT

OBJECTIVES

- Before obtaining credit, you should:
- Explain how credit affects your personal and business finances
- Identify the three Cs of credit.
- Explain the advantages and disadvantages of buying on credit
- Determine the long-term effect of good and bad credit.

WARM-UP

1. James borrowed $13,000 to purchase a car. He paid off the loan in five years. At the end of five years, he had paid the bank $14,630. How much interest did he pay?

_____

_____

_____

_____

_____

TIP: A credit score is a number that will be attached to your name for your entire life once you buy using credit. The higher the score, the more financial opportunities there will be available to you. Try to keep it above 750. A score of over 800 is very good.

LESSON HIGHLIGHTS

Credit has many definitions. Credit is confidence in a buyer's or borrower's ability to pay their financial obligations. It can be an arrangement for a person or business to buy goods now and pay later. Credit is the amount placed by a bank at a borrower's disposal. Credit is also payment made on a loan to reduce the amount owed on the loan. All these definitions affect the way we achieve personal goals and business success.

When determining who is eligible for credit, one formula known as the **three Cs of credit** is used:

1. Character- Does the borrower have an honest reputation?
2. Capacity - Based on borrower's income and expenses, can the borrower repay?
3. Capital – What are the borrower's physical and financial assets or collateral?

Good credit will help you obtain a college education, a car loan, a home mortgage, and money to grow a business. Good credit allows you to book hotels and rent cars when taking vacations. Most sales over the internet are done using credit cards. Good credit allows you to enjoy a good life and pay much less interest than someone with poor credit.

Remember that credit is a loan that must be repaid on time. By not paying these loans on time and having too many credit cards you stand the risk of getting a low or poor credit score. Your credit score affects most things you want to do financially. It may even affect your ability to get a job, buy a home, or buy a car. Bad credit can also lead to unwanted stress and poor health

ACTIVITY

Write three conclusions that can be drawn from information presented in this lesson.

1.

_____

_____

_____

_____

_____

_____

_____

2.

_____

_____

_____

_____

_____

_____

_____

_____

3.

_____

_____

_____

_____

_____

_____

_____

NEXT MEETING

Visit a local bank and find out what are the requirements to open a checking or savings account.

UNIT 3
TOPIC 6 BANKING

OBJECTIVES

In order to reach your financial goals and acquire wealth you should:

- Establish a relationship with a bank by maintaining an account.
- Become familiar with the different types of accounts and services offered by banks.

WARM-UP

Why is a budget important when setting financial goals?

_____

_____

_____

_____

_____

_____

_____

_____

_____

_____

LESSON HIGHLIGHTS

BANKS PURPOSE

Banks are institutions established for the purpose of holding money for individuals, corporations, and governments. They pay interest for the use of this money. They also loan money to other individuals, corporations, and governments at a higher rate of interest than they pay to make a profit. Banks also invest this money in securities (stocks and bonds).

BANKING SERVICES

Banks today offer services for all your financial transactions. They offer a variety of checking, savings, credit cards, and investment accounts.

Checking accounts enable you to write checks as a form of payment based on the amount of money you have in your account. This account also allows you to use an automatic teller machine (ATM). There are different types of checking accounts, some of which pay a small amount of interest.

Savings accounts usually require a minimum balance. Sometimes savings accounts are linked to checking accounts to make it easier to transfer money between the two accounts. The interest the bank pays you for this account varies from bank to bank. Therefore, it is good to shop around for the best rate.

INTEREST

Interest is the cost of using or borrowing money. It is the amount the bank pays you for the use of your money or charges you for lending you money. The amount depends on a rate or percentage which is tied to the prime interest rate tied to the financial markets and the Federal Reserve Bank.

$$\text{Interest} = \text{Principal} \times \text{Rate} \times \text{Time}$$

Example: Calculate the interest paid on a $12,000 loan at 5% for 4 years.
Answer: Interest = 12,000 x .05 x4 = $2,400.00

ONLINE BANKING

Online banking provides the ability to do 24-hour banking using the internet and various electronic devices. It is sometimes called home banking or web banking. Customers can check bank balances, pay bills, transfer money between accounts, apply for mortgages, and use direct deposit to have payroll checks deposited into our account.

PAYMENT NETWORKS

Over the past several years banks have created apps for customers to quickly send and receive money from their bank account to someone else's bank account. Zelle, PayPal, Venmo, Cash App, Apple Pay, and Google Pay are some of the more popular apps.

ACTIVITY

1. Calculate the interest paid on a $52,000 Audi over 3 years at an 8% interest rate.

    _____

    _____

    _____

    _____

    _____

    _____

    _____

2. What is the total amount paid for the Audi at the end of 3 years

    _____

    _____

    _____

    _____

    _____

    _____

    _____

UNIT 4

TOPIC 7
INTRODUCTION TO THE STOCK MARKET

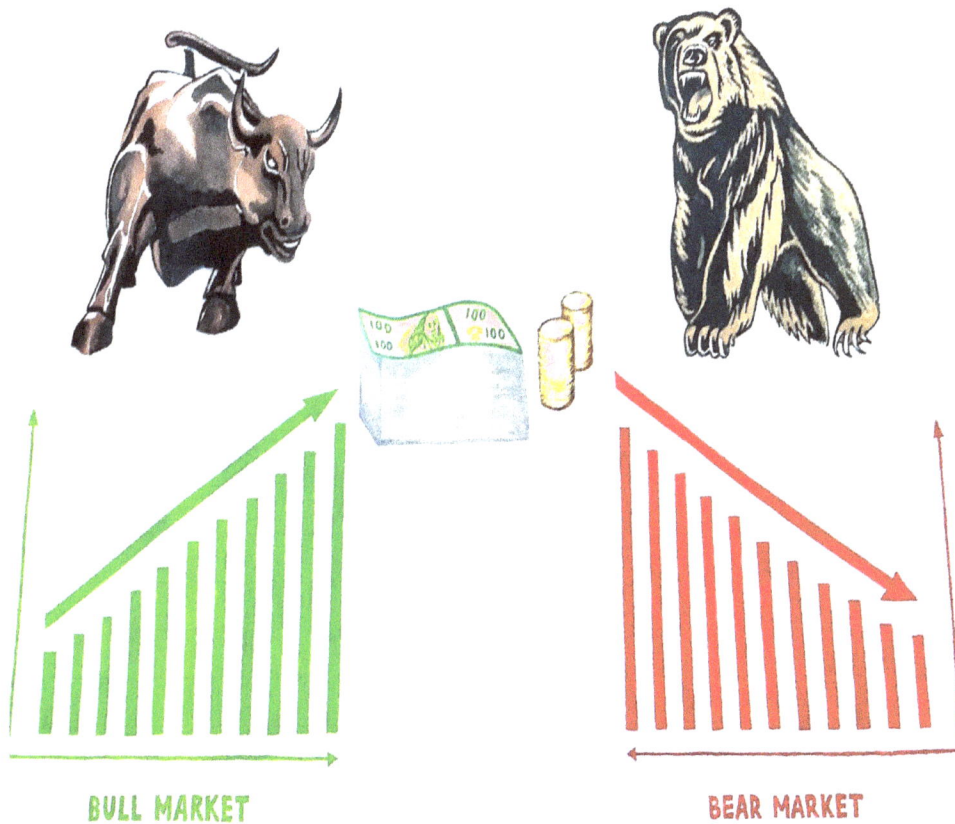

BULL MARKET

BEAR MARKET

OBJECTIVES

1. Explain the purpose of stocks and the rights of a stockholder or shareholder.
2. Identify the purpose of exchanges and brokerages.
3. Name 5 top stock exchanges.
4. Explain the purpose of stock indices.
5. Name 5 top stock indices
6. Name some categories in which stocks are grouped.
7. Identify the information on a stock ticker tape.
8. What do the bear and bull represent?

WARM-UP

1. Identify 5 copies in which you would like to own stock.

_____

_____

_____

_____

_____

_____

_____

2. List the most recent price for which each is selling.

_____

_____

_____

_____

_____

_____

_____

LESSON HIGHLIGHTS

A private company will go public when money or capital is needed to grow or expand sales. A company will sell shares in the company.

Shares or **stock** represent partial ownership or equity in the company. Stockholders or Shareholders purchase shares of stock and attend annual shareholders meetings where they can vote on company issues.

INTERPRETING A DAILY STOCK QUOTATION

Below is a daily stock quotation:

NIKE   99.16 98.49 88.66 128.68

The current price of a share of Nike stock is $99.16. Yesterday at the close of the market the price for one share was $98.49. Over the past year (52 Weeks) the lowest price for one share of Nike stock was $88.66 and the highest price for one share over the past year was $128.68. Different publications may present this information in another order and possibly add more data.

BULL VS BEAR MARKET

BULL MARKET – PRICES OF STOCKS ARE GOING UP(BUY)

BEAR Market – PRICES OF STOCKS ARE GOING DOWN(SELL)

Stocks are purchased by investors through brokerage houses or investment banks. Charles Schwab, Edward Jones, and Merrill Lynch are well known investment companies. Stocks may also be purchased at online brokerages such as E*Trade, Charles Schwab, Sofi, and Fidelity.

Investment banks or brokerages purchase stocks on exchanges. The price of stock is reported daily on a ticker tape at different exchanges, such as the New York Stock Exchange (NYSE) and National Association of Securities Dealers Automated Quotations (NASDAQ).

Its reporting is done on what is referred to as the **Big Board**. Exchanges not only report the current price of stock but also the previous twelve months' highest and lowest prices. You want to purchase when the stock price is low and sell when it is high. Many countries have their own stock exchanges.

What to know before making a stock purchase

Before purchasing stock, you must do your homework and learn something about the company and its products or services. You must know its market (who it sells to) and what its cash flow and balance sheet look like. This information can be found in its **annual report**. You should also know what stock analysts predict for the company's future. Also find out if the company recently paid a **dividend** (a portion of the profits) to its shareholders. Dividends are usually paid out quarterly.

MOST WELL-KNOWN STOCK INDICES

- DOW JONES INDUSTRIAL AVERAGE (DJIA) consists of 30 major companies in diversified industries such as retail, technology, healthcare, banking, etc.
- NATIONAL ASSOCIATION OF SECURITIES DEALERS AUTOMATED QUOTATIONS(NASDAQ) is a computerized system that quotes volume of securities traded over the counter (OTC) or on other exchanges. It lists over 5,000 companies and is divided into two markets, one for large companies and one for small emerging companies.
- STANDARD AND POORS (S&P) is a company that rates stocks according to risk. The S&P 500 is an index of the 500 largest capitalized companies in the United States.
- NIKKEI is a stock market index for the Tokyo Stock Exchange.

Types of Stocks

There are all types of stocks and combinations of stocks. The following represent some of the basic types:

- **Common Stock** is partial ownership in the company
- **Preferred Stock** pays higher dividends than common stock and has voting privileges attached. These shareholders are paid before common shareholders especially if the company goes bankrupt or out of business.
- **Convertible Stocks** are preferred stocks which can be converted to common stocks.
- **Initial Public Offering (IPO)** is first time issued stock to the public to help finance a company's growth
- **Exchange Traded Funds (ETF)** is a type of investment that bundles groups of similar stocks, bonds, or commodities. They trade like individual stocks on the stock exchanges.
- **Non-Fungible Token (NFT)** is a digital asset which represents ownership of a specific item. This item could be virtual real estate, artwork, videos, and music. It is unique. They are bought in online marketplaces using cryptocurrency.

BONDS

When you purchase a bond, you are making a loan to a government or corporation for a period (usually 1 to 10 years). This bond has an interest rate and a **maturity date** which tells when the money is due. Bonds are not as risky as stocks and government bonds offer the greatest security. The longer the date to maturity, the higher the interest rate will rise. Bonds make regular interest payments up until they mature. This interest is known as **fixed income**.

Types of Bonds

Bonds differ based on who is issuing the bond, their credit worthiness, maturity date which could be as long as ten years, and interest rate. Interest is usually paid semi-annually. The price of a bond also varies inversely with interest rates. The higher the interest rate the lower the price of bonds. The **Federal Reserve Bank** (**The Fed**) establishes the prime interest rate which is usually the lowest rate.

Types of Bonds usually available are:

- U.S. Government
- State and municipal
- Mortgage-Backed
- Corporate
- Junk Bonds which have low credit ratings.

Certificates of Deposit

Certificates of deposit are long-term savings accounts that pay the highest interest rates and are backed by the Federal Government (FDIC) if the bank should fail. They offer the least risk.

MUTUAL FUNDS

Mutual funds are investments which combine diverse investment vehicles and are held by a group of people who have common financial goals. These funds are watched over by professional money managers. The investors share in the cost and the profits of these accounts. Because these funds are held by a group, there is less risk

DIVERSIFICATION

Most experienced investors have a **portfolio** which contains a variety of stocks, bonds, saving certificates, and mutual funds. They constantly depend on financial experts to track these investments.

By diversifying one's portfolio, it reduces risk or the chance of losing money.

ACTIVITIES

1. Select 2 long term financial goals and explain the importance of saving and investing to achieve these goals.

_____

_____

_____

2. Select 3 companies listed on the NYSE and compare information on their daily stock report.

_____

_____

_____

3. Track these 3 companies for a week. Based on their performance, are they currently a good or bad investments.

_____

_____

_____

4. Go online and identify three mutual funds and summarize what securities they invest in.

_____

_____

_____

5. Identify 4 ETFs and some of assets they contain.

_____

_____

_____

6. Research 4 NFTs and give the current value.

_____

_____

_____

UNIT 5

ENTREPRENEURSHIP

TOPIC 8
RECOGNIZING BUSINESS OPPORTUNITIES

OBJECTIVES

Students will be able to:

- Identify elements of creative thinking
- Discuss meaning of "thinking out of the box."
- Investigate places to look for inspiration
- Identify and explore current business trends
- Identify famous entrepreneurs and what factors contributed to their success.

ESSENTIAL QUESTION

How does thinking creatively support business opportunities?

_____
_____
_____
_____
_____
_____
_____
_____
_____
_____

LESSON HIGHLIGHTS

The dictionary defines opportunity as a favorable or promising combination of circumstances which provide a good chance for advancement or progress. In business an opportunity has commercial value. We are always looking for opportunities to expand our business by increasing sales and profits. We usually do this by making improvements to existing products and services. We must think about the needs of our customers. What improvements can be made to increase our customer base and make the company a leader in its industry?

To take advantage of opportunity, we must learn to think creatively. When we think creatively, we use our imagination to rise above or transcend traditional ideas, methods, patterns, rules, products, relationships, etc., and produce something new. This process is also referred to as "thinking out of the box." We also use a technique called "brainstorming", where ideas are given without being judged as good or bad, right or wrong.

The elements of creativity are connection, discovery, invention, and application. We connect things that are usually not connected. Cookie dough and ice cream are examples of this process.

To get inspired to think creatively, you must first stop and observe the world around you. Look at people when you are in the mall, in a park, or at a game.

Describe the personal characteristics of the people you encounter. These characteristics are called **demographics** and include gender, race, culture, income, education, and ethnicity. Also read newspapers and magazines to get ideas. Finally, use the internet.

What is an entrepreneur?

An **entrepreneur** is a person who creates, organizes, operates, and owns a business. They assume the financial risk and responsibilities in starting and running a new business or **venture**. To start a business requires many skills which will be explored in this handbook.

Entrepreneurship is the process of identifying a potential business, finding and testing it on potential customers, and obtaining the financing to start the business.

To help develop new business opportunities, you must identify current business trends. The biggest trends today are e-business and e-commerce which use the internet. Almost every field including retail sales, education, finance, and publishing does business on the internet. Also, social media businesses such as fashion and entertainment blogs, as well as podcasts have proved to be financially successful. Developing medical, dating, and game apps is popular. Service businesses such as fitness centers, pet grooming, food catering, and wedding planning are on the rise. Many new entrepreneurs choose **franchising** when starting their own business. When you purchase a franchise, you become the owner of an outpost of a larger company, Stanley Steamer, MacDonalds, and Comfort Inn are examples of franchise businesses.

When purchasing a franchise, you purchase a territory and franchisor's business system, which includes accounting, advertising, and procedures.

Finally, if we look at the lives of some famous entrepreneurs such as Jeff Bezos (Amazon), Elon Musk (Tesla and SpaceX), Bill Gates (Microsoft), Tyler Perry (Tyler Perry Studios), Oprah Winfrey (OWN), Warren Buffett (Berkshire Hathaway), and Mark Zuckerberg (Facebook), we find that their environments and interest provided the inspiration for their success.

ACTIVITIES

1. Identify two additional current business trends and their products. Write a short paragraph on each.

   _____

   _____

   _____

   _____

   _____

   _____

   _____

2. Use the internet to identify 5 e-commerce businesses and give their web addresses. Include a business related to sports.

   _____

   _____

   _____

   _____

   _____

   _____

   _____

   _____

TOPIC 9
TEAM BUILDING

OBJECTIVES

Athlete will be able to:

- Identify the key characteristics of a good team
- Develop interviewing skills
- Define and analyze factors influencing wages

ESSENTIAL QUESTION

How does choosing a good team impact the success of a business?

_____

_____

_____

_____

_____

_____

_____

_____

WARM-UP

List the elements of creative thinking

_____

_____

_____

_____

_____

_____

_____

_____

LESSON HIGHLIGHTS

1. Team building/Teamwork

Just as in sports, team building is essential to the success of operating a business. A sports or business **team** consists of two or more people organized to work together to accomplish a task or reach a common goal. Winning a sports championship is a common goal. Teams bring together the skills and knowledge of its members. Working at Burger King uses the work team concept. Each person on the team has a responsibility. The responsibility could be counting inventory; displaying inventory; preparing food; cleaning and maintenance; serving customers; handling money; or keeping financial records. There should also be a manager to make sure all tasks are completed in a timely manner.

The following are some general characteristics of a good team:

- A clear goal or mission which everyone accepts
- Willing participation by every member
- Open and relaxed communication between members
- Clear understanding of work assignments
- Resolve problems on a timely basis
- Use listening skills by focusing on the speaker
- Recognize that disagreements will arise but remain respectful of each other.
- Regular evaluation of the team's performance to see if work can be done better.

2. Interviewing

Before being considered for any job, the job seeker must complete a job application and a job interview. For many jobs there may be several stages until an actual face to face interview. This is especially true for professional jobs and applications online. The company may receive thousands of applications. To narrow the number of applicants, the first interview may be via phone. There may be a second interview via Skype or FaceTime. The final job interview enables the employer to have face-to-face contact to see if the applicant fits into the culture of a particular workplace. The interview also allows the applicant to tell why they are the best person for the job.

The following are guidelines for a successful interview:

- Dress appropriately, good grooming and hygiene matter. Check your body language. Keep your hands in your lap. Do not sit back with your arms folded.
- Research the company. You should know such things as what they produce and who their competitors are.
- Be courteous and polite.
- Ask questions to the interviewer about job responsibilities and training
- Be prepared to answer common interview questions such as:
  a. Why do you want this job?
  b. Can you tell us something about yourself?
  c. What is your greatest strength.

After the interview, thank the interviewer for their time and effort.

3. Factors influencing wage

A **wage** is the amount of money one receives for every hour worked. Thus, the wage is expressed as a rate- $9.00/hr., or $8.75 per hour. A **pay** or **total earnings** is the amount received for a pay period. The period could be weekly, biweekly, twice a month, or monthly. The hours worked are recorded on a time sheet and the pay is shown on a payroll stub.

<u>Example</u>: Anthony worked 35 hours this week and earns $9.50 per hour. What are his total earnings?

<u>Answer</u>: $9.50 x 35 = $332.50

Thus, wages or pay are influenced by the hourly rate and the hours worked.

Gross pay is the total amount earned during a pay period. Net pay (take-home pay) is the amount left after federal, state, local taxes, social security (FICA), and disability insurance (SDI) are deducted from the gross pay.

ACTIVITIES

1. Identify additional characteristics you desire in a good team member.

   _____

   _____

   _____

   _____

   _____

2. Create a poster on all the characteristics of a good team member.

   _____

   _____

   _____

   _____

   _____

3. Students practice job interviewing by pairing off. One person will represent the employer and the other will play the job applicant. They will later reverse roles. If possible, this activity should be videotaped.

   _____

   _____

   _____

   _____

   _____

4. Complete the timecard for several employees, given the hours worked daily.

TIMECARD

Employee #

Employee Name:

Week Ending _____ **20**____

	A.M.		P.M.	Hours	
	In	Out	In	Out	Worked
Mon.					
Tues.					
Wed.					
Thurs.					
Fri.					
Sat.					
Sun.					

5. Complete the earnings portion of the following pay stub given:

Regular hours -40
Overtime hours -6
Regular pay rate -$8.50
Overtime rate – time and a half (1.5 x regular rate).

PAY STUB
EARNINGS

WEEK ENDING	PAY RATE	REGULAR PAY	OVER TIME HOURS	REGULAR PAY	OVER TIME PAY	GROSS PAY	

DEDUCTIONS							
FICA	FWT	STATE TAX	LOCAL TAX	SDI	OTHER	TOTAL DEDUCTIONS	NET PAY

WRAP-UP

Present pros and cons of why a potential employer should be able to view your Facebook, Twitter, or Instagram accounts.

_____

_____

_____

_____

_____

_____

_____

_____

_____

_____

TOPIC 10
MANAGING BUSINESS FINANCES

OBJECTIVES

- *Become familiar with various types of financial statements*
- Collect data necessary to complete a spreadsheet
- Prepare an income, cash flow, and balance sheet using monthly data collected from a business such as the school store.

ESSENTIAL QUESTION

How is data used to forecast business operations?

_____
_____
_____
_____
_____
_____
_____
_____
_____
_____

WARM-UP

What is the difference between gross pay and net pay?

_____
_____
_____
_____
_____
_____
_____
_____

LESSON HIGHLIGHTS

STEPS FOR PREPARING A BUSINESS BUDGET

1. List all income or revenue. This includes income from wages or sales and income from bonuses or investments.

   _____

   _____

   _____

2. List all **fixed expenses** such as rent, mortgages, car payments, insurances, internet, trash, property taxes, etc. These expenses are about the same each month.

   _____

   _____

   _____

3. List **variable expenses** such as entertainment, gifts, supplies and employee wages.

   _____

   _____

   _____

4. Calculate the difference between total income and total expenses.

   _____

   _____

   _____

5. Adjust if there are more expenses than income which represents a **net loss**.

   _____

   _____

   _____

6. Periodically compare budgeted amounts with the actual amounts. A **spreadsheet** can be used to make this comparison for several months or a year.

   _____

   _____

   _____

Other Types of Financial Statements

- **Income Statement** – A report which shows the revenue and expenses for the period. It also shows net income or net loss.

- **Cash Flow Statement** – A report which shows what cash was taken in and what cash was disbursed (paid out). It also shows net cash flow.

- **Balance Sheet** – A report which shows all **assets** (cash, equipment, supplies, and **account receivables** (money owed to your business). The balance sheet also shows all **liabilities** which include **accounts payable** (money you owe to suppliers) and notes payable (money you borrowed). Finally, the balance sheet shows **the owner's equity** (total assets minus total liabilities). Examples of the financial statements are in the appendix at the back of this handbook.

ACTIVITIES

Research and list websites which assist in developing budgets and financial statements such as www.creditkarma.com.

_____

_____

_____

_____

_____

_____

_____

_____

_____

_____

WRAP-UP

Using Glogster.com or Canvasteria.com create a poster for a product you would like to advertise.

_____

_____

_____

_____

_____

_____

_____

_____

_____

_____

TOPIC 11
THE BUSINESS PLAN

OBJECTIVES

- Explain the purpose and importance of a business plan
- Identify and explain the key elements of a business plan
- Create a business plan

ESSENTIAL QUESTION

How does the development of a sound business plan impact the success of a new business?

_____

_____

_____

_____

_____

_____

_____

_____

WARM-UP

Develop an argument for portfolio diversification.

_____

_____

_____

_____

_____

_____

_____

_____

LESSON HIGHLIGHTS

THE BUSINESS PLAN

Once a new entrepreneur has decided on a potential business venture, developing a business plan is crucial to its success. The **business plan** is a document which describes in detail a new business and it operational strategies. It also looks at costs associated with the business and helps discover any problems that may exist when starting up the business.

The business plan is crucial because it is reviewed by potential partners, investors, management, and banks. Thus it is the key document when trying to obtain funding for startup costs.

BUSINESS PLAN COMPONENTS

Developing a business plan requires a great deal of research on all aspects of the new business. The plan's real value comes in that it forces the business owner to do research and think thoroughly about the business in a systematic and logical way. Planning now avoids failure later. Most business plans have the following general components.

Executive Summary

This component gives a summary of the plan. It should be no more than two pages. It should include a paragraph as to why the business is going to be successful and what is the outlook for the business and the industry. Statistics and evidence gathered through market research should also be included to support your statements.

Also include a description of the product, the targeted customer, and the owners. If presenting the plan to bankers or investors, include how much money is needed to make the company profitable and how the money will be used. **The executive summary should be written last.**

Company Summary

Identifies the company and gives a concise explanation of the business. It also includes historical information about the business. The location of the business and why the business will succeed is also included.

Products and Services (Marketing Plan)

This section describes the products and services offered by the business as well as future products and services. You should focus on customer benefits. Identify the competition and why your company is better and different. The marketing plan is developed more thoroughly in Topic 12.

Industry Overview

You can find information on your industry by using a search engine (e.g. music recording, jewelry, or fashion design). This section should include industry sales figures in terms of dollars and number of units sold. Any other statistics such as the number of employees should also be included. ChatGPT I with AI(Artificial Intelligence) can be helpful as a search engine.

Competitor Analysis

The first step in your analysis is to research and identify your competition. This includes your direct competition making the same product as you and your indirect competition who offer substitute products that will satisfy the customer's needs. In the restaurant industry you have different levels of eat-in restaurants and fast-food restaurants. In the retail industry you have department stores, boutiques, and specialty stores.

In your analysis you should include:

1. Name and location of your competitors
2. Who do they serve?
3. What is their product or specialty?
4. How long have they been in business?
5. What is their sales volume?
6. What advantage do you have over your competition?

Operation Plan

The operation plan describes the location of the business, and the equipment needed to operate the business. It describes the production process and if any of the production will be outsourced or done by outside vendors or contractors. Who supplies your business should be mentioned in this plan.

Quality safeguards should also be included as well as what procedures will be used to keep cost down and still provide a quality product. When considering the labor supply, how accessible business is to transportation should also be included.

Electronic businesses (E-business) should include a description of the website and how it works and how it will be used. You may also want to mention security safeguards and social networks used.

Organization Plan

This component describes the organization and its structure. It identifies the members of the management team, their qualifications, and position. A resume for each person should be included as well as a description of their responsibilities in the company. Also include the management philosophy and whether the company is a corporation, partnership, or limited liability.

If there are any partnership agreements, they should also be included.

Financial Plan

The financial plan is a quantitative analysis to determine future profits. This plan helps you prepare your business for the years ahead. If you need outside funding, this is one of the first sections bankers and investors will review.

The financial plan shows how much money is needed to start and operate the business. It also shows how sales goals will be met.

The financial plan has three main sections:

- Statement of revenue sources and how they will be used indicates the amount of **capital** or money needed to get the business up and running.

- Pro forma financial statements show projections as to when the company will become profitable. It includes a cash flow statement, income statement and a balance sheet. These statements were discussed in Topic 3.
- The third section is a financial analysis which compares your business to the industry standard and indicates a **breakeven point** (point when the revenue equals the expenses).

Growth Plan

Every business needs a plan to grow and stay competitive. Once the business is started what is going to be done to ensure continued growth and profits over many years. What strategies will be used to help the business succeed?

Four strategies investors are interested in are:

- **Product Development** which will include new products or enhancing existing products
- **Market Development** which reaches out to new markets which could be in other countries
- **Market Penetration** which requires selling to more customers or getting customers to buy more of your product.
- **Diversification** involves selling new products in a different market. This is a very risky strategy since you are leaving a market with which you are familiar.

Timing and costs are key factors when deciding on strategy.

Risk Management Plan

In today's economic environment business may not go as we planned. There are financial risks, market risks, time-loss risks, and political risks. Energy costs, change in customer taste, technology innovations, extreme weather conditions are examples of risks.

A successful business identifies their possible risks and develops a strategy plan to operate around these risks.

Having business insurance will minimize these risks.

Plan Layout

VII.	Cover Page – Include name of company, date name of highest officer, company address, phone, fax number, email, and date.
VIII.	Table of Contents
IX.	Executive Summary
X.	Company Summary
XI.	Industry Overview
XII.	Competitor Analysis
XIII.	Operational Plan
XIV.	Organizational Plan
XV.	Financial Plan
XVI.	Marketing Plan
XVII.	Growth Plan
XVIII.	Risk Management Plan
XIX.	Appendix – Includes financial reports

ACTIVITIES

Select a business and research and write an industry overview.

_____

_____

_____

_____

_____

_____

_____

_____

_____

_____

TOPIC 12
MARKETING

OBJECTIVES

Students will be able to:

- Layout and evaluate a marketing plan
- Discuss the impact of false advertising on a business

ESSENTIAL QUESTION

How does a good marketing strategy impact a business?

_____

_____

_____

_____

_____

_____

_____

WARM-UP

Identify and explain two components of a business plan.

_____

_____

_____

_____

_____

_____

_____

LESSON HIGHLIGHTS

Definition

The American Marketing Association defines **marketing** as an activity, set of institutions, and processes for creating, communicating, delivering, and exchanging offerings that have value for customers, clients, partners, and society. This is not the only definition.

Because the way business is conducted is ever- changing, the definition of marketing is ever-evolving. Marketing is used to identify, satisfy, and keep the customer. Marketing management is a major component in any business management program. Today many universities view it as a science because in dealing with the issue of selling to a customer, companies must design a plan that uses psychology, sociology, mathematics, economics, statistics, and a few other sciences.

Thus, it is a major component in an entrepreneurship program. How are items marketed in the school store or sports concession stand to increase sales, product awareness, customer satisfaction, and repeat customers?

Marketing Objectives are the results a company wants to accomplish through its marketing campaign. The objectives for a new business should be clear, concise, measurable, and easily controlled.

When listing these objectives they should include the following:

- Introduction of the new product or enhancements and innovations to existing product.
- An organizational description of the team.
- Projected sales or market share
- Projected profits
- How the product or service will be priced
- What are the distribution channels? These include delivery terms, shipping, receiving, handling, storage, and warehousing.
- Advertising (media or print)

Marketing Orientation and Strategies

Market orientation refers to the way a company feels about its product or service. **Market strategies** are plans of action for getting the product or service to the consumer. **Market mix** refers to a combination of strategies used to reach the consumer.

Over the years marketing orientation or how a company feels about its product has changed. In the early years marketing focused on one of the following orientations:

- Production – Company produces as much as possible because of high demand for the product. An example is car production in the late 1940's and 1950's.
- Product - Company focuses on producing a quality product because consumer has high standards. Luxury cars, watches and handbags are examples.
- Selling – Company tries to sell as much as possible using varies promotion techniques. This is used when a product is in high demand. A good example of this strategy is lower priced pizza and televisions at the start of the football season.

Recent approaches in market orientation focus on the needs and tastes of the consumer. These approaches use market research. They also use Research and Development (R&D) to create new and improved products.

A few of these approaches include:

- Relationship Marketing- maintaining good customer relationships
- Business Marketing – focus is selling to other businesses
- Social Marketing – there is a benefit to the whole society
- Internet Marketing- marketing via email, online, search engine, desktop, and affiliate, and QR codes or Quick Response codes.

Marketing Strategies are long term or multiple year plans for dealing with the development and growth of a product. Earlier strategies consisted of the 4P's, product, place, price, and promotion. In recent years a fifth P has emerged which deals with people. Some strategies deal with market dominance, product differentiation, and how innovative is the product. Many times, a company may use a combination of these strategies called a **market mix**.

Today online marketing strategies enable businesses to quickly reach a larger market. Social media such as Twitter, Tumblr, Facebook, Pinterest and Instagram can have a major impact on sales because of their global audience.

Marketing Plans are one of the foundations for having a successful business. It is the plan used to accomplish marketing objectives, reach the target market or customer, and grow the business.

The market plan is developed based on market research and if developed properly can be used to convince investors and banks to help provide funding.

Market Plan Components consist of the following:

- Executive Summary – focuses on marketing objectives, budget, and business projections.
- Business Overview – gives information on the state of industry, competitors, strengths, and weaknesses of the industry.
- Target Market – profiles the customer who will purchase product.
- Marketing Objectives - identifies the goals or what the plan is to accomplish.
- Tactics or Action Plan – states how the business will be advertised over a given time frame.
- Market Strategies – gives the mix of strategies that will be used to meet objectives. It also identifies the tasks that must be completed and identifies who is responsible for each task.
- Budget – gives the cost of operating the business and the anticipated revenue.

ACTIVITIES

1. Research and identify several marketing strategies that are popular today.

   _____

   _____

   _____

   _____

   _____

2. Identify an online strategy that is used and companies who use it.

   _____

   _____

   _____

   _____

   _____

3. Explain the 5P's of marketing.

   _____

   _____

   _____

   _____

   _____

APPENDICES

A   **Personal Monthly Budget**

B   **Sample Consolidated Balance Sheet**

C   **Sample Monthly Income Statement**

D   **Sample Monthly Statement of Cash Flow**

APPENDIX A

Personal Monthly Budget   Month _____ Year

INCOME:

Wages/Tips	$ 5,280.00
Interest income	$ 2.00
Other Income	$ 250.00
Total Income	$ 5,532.00

EXPENSES:

Savings	$ 200.00
Rent/Mortgage	$ 1,670.00
Health Insurance	$ 320.00
Car Payment	$ 360.00
Car Insurance	$ 225.00
Utilities	$ 230.00
Phone	$ 146.00
Cable	$ 87.00
Credit Cards/Store Accounts	$ 180.00
School Loans	$ 260.00
Groceries	$ 400.00
Transportation/Gas	$ 230.00
Laundry/Cleaners	$ 128.00
Clothing/Hair Allowance	$ 225.00
Entertainment	$ 240.00
Gifts	$ 5.00
Other Expenses	$ 200.00
Total Expenses	$ 5,106.00

NET INCOME	$ 426.00

APPENDIX B

Easy Corporation
Consolidated Balance Sheet
December 31, 20___

Assets
Current Assets:

Cash or Cash Equivalents	$ 40,750
Accounts and notes receivables	$ 68,500
Inventories at lower of cost	$ 91,750
Prepaid expenses	$ 7,000
Total current assets	$ 208,000

Investments:

Bonds	$ 42,250
Dividends from stocks	$ 24,000
Total Investments	$ 66,250

Fixed Assets:

Land	$ 25,000
Buildings	$ 92,000

B-1

Machinery and equipment	$ 199,820
Total Fixed Assets	$ 316,200

Intangible Assets:

Goodwill	$ 55,000
Total Assets	$ 645,450

Liabilities

Current Liabilities:

Accounts Payable	$ 63,284
Income Tax Payable	$ 14,666
Dividends Payable	$ 5,000
Accrued l Liabilities	$ 9,410
Total Current Liabilities	$ 92,360

Long-term Liabilities:

Bonds Payable	$ 34,000
Total Long-term Liabilitie	$ 34,000
Deferred income taxes payable	$ 7,790
Total Liabilities	$ 134,150
Stockholders' Equity	$ 511,300
Total Liabilities and Stockholders Equity	$ 645,450

APPENDIX C

XYZ Travel Service
Income Statement
For the Month Ended October 31, 20___

Fees earned	$ 8,300.00
Expenses:	
Wages expense	$ 3,725.00
Rent expense	$ 1,450.00
Utilities expense	$ 980.00
Supplies Expense	$ 875.00
Miscellaneous expense	$ 640.00
Total expenses	$ 7,670.00
Net income	$ 630.00

Appendix D

XYZ Travel Service

Statement of Cash Flows

For the Month Ended October 31, 2012

Cash flows from operating activities:

Cash received from customers	$ 8,300.00
Deduct cash payments for expenses and payments to creditors	$ 7,740.00
Net cash flows from operating activities	$ 560.00

Cash flows from investing activities:

Cash payments for purchase of building	(32,000.00)

Cash flows from financing activities:

Cash received from issuing stock	$ 40,000.00
Deduct cash dividends	$ 2,600.00
Net cash flows from financing	$ 37,400.00

Net cash flow as of October 31, 20___	$ 5,960.00

www.ingramcontent.com/pod-product-compliance
Lightning Source LLC
Chambersburg PA
CBHW081824200326
41597CB00023B/4379